Famous Lives/Vidas extraordinarias

The Life of
Abraham Lincoln/
La vida de
Abraham Lincoln

By Maria Nelson   Traducción al español: Eduardo Alamán

Gareth Stevens
Publishing

Please visit our website, www.garethstevens.com. For a free color catalog of all our high-quality books, call toll free 1-800-542-2595 or fax 1-877-542-2596.

Library of Congress Cataloging-in-Publication Data

Nelson, Maria.
[Life of Abraham Lincoln. Spanish & English]
The life of Abraham Lincoln = La vida de Abraham Lincoln / Maria Nelson.
    p. cm. — (Famous lives = Vidas extraordinarias)
Includes index.
ISBN 978-1-4339-6651-4 (library binding)
1. Lincoln, Abraham, 1809-1865—Juvenile literature. 2. Presidents—United States—Biography—Juvenile literature. I. Title. II. Title: Vida de Abraham Lincoln.
E457.905.N4518 2012
973.7092—dc23
[B]
                                    2011038179

First Edition

Published in 2012 by
Gareth Stevens Publishing
111 East 14th Street, Suite 349
New York, NY 10003

Copyright © 2012 Gareth Stevens Publishing

Designer: Daniel Hosek
Editor: Kristen Rajczak
Spanish translation: Eduardo Alamán

Photo credits: Cover, pp. 1, 5, 21 Stock Montage/Getty Images; pp. 7, 13 George Eastman House/Getty Images; p. 9 Hulton Archive/Stock Montage/Getty Images; p. 11 Buyenlarge/Getty Images; pp. 15, 17, 19 SuperStock/Masterfile.com.

Printed in the United States of America

CPSIA compliance information: Batch #CW12GS: For further information contact Gareth Stevens, New York, New York at 1-800-542-2595.

Contents

Contenido

Boldface words appear in the glossary/
Las palabras en **negrita** aparecen en el glosario

A Great Man

Abraham Lincoln was the 16th president of the United States. Many people say he was the greatest president! Lincoln was a very good speaker and leader. His actions helped free African Americans from **slavery**.

Un gran hombre

Abraham Lincoln fue el decimosexto presidente de los Estados Unidos. ¡Para muchos, Lincoln ha sido el mejor presidente! Lincoln era un gran líder y orador. El trabajo de Lincoln contribuyó a terminar con la **esclavitud** de los afroamericanos.

Growing Up

Lincoln was born in Kentucky on February 12, 1809. His family moved to Indiana in 1816 and to Illinois in 1830. Lincoln didn't go to school but learned to read and write. He studied law and became a lawyer.

Primeros años

Lincoln nació el 12 de febrero de 1809, en Kentucky. Su familia se mudó a Indiana en 1816 y a Illinois en 1830. Lincoln no asistió a la escuela pero aprendió a leer y escribir. Lincoln estudió leyes y se convirtió en abogado.

Family

Lincoln married Mary Todd in 1842. They had four sons. Edward and William died very young. The others were named Robert and Thomas.

Familia

Lincoln se casó con Mary Todd en 1842. La pareja tuvo cuatro hijos. Edward y William murieron muy jóvenes. Los otros dos se llamaban Robert y Thomas.

Leader

Lincoln was **elected** to the US **House of Representatives** in 1847. He ran for US Senate in 1858. He lost, but many people thought he was a good speaker.

Un líder

Lincoln fue **elegido** para la **Cámara de Representantes** en 1847. Lincoln se postuló para el Senado en 1858. Lincoln no ganó, pero muchas personas pensaron que era un gran orador.

The Election of 1860

Lincoln was elected US president in 1860. Before he took office, South Carolina **seceded** from the United States. More states followed. They were worried that Lincoln would outlaw slavery. These states formed the Confederate States of America.

- - - - - - - - - - -

La elección de 1860

Lincoln fue elegido presidente de los Estados Unidos en 1860. Antes de asumir la presidencia, Carolina del Sur se **separó** de los Estados Unidos. Otros estados hicieron lo mismo porque les preocupaba que Lincoln prohibiera la esclavitud. Estos estados formaron los Estados Confederados.

Civil War

Lincoln wanted to keep the United States together. He was willing to go to war to do this. The American **Civil War** began in 1861. Then, Lincoln had to take a stand on slavery.

Guerra Civil

Lincoln quería mantener unidos a los Estados Unidos. Para esto, Lincoln estaba dispuesto a declarar la guerra. La **Guerra Civil** comenzó en 1861. Entonces, Lincoln tuvo que tomar una posición sobre la esclavitud.

A Proclamation

On January 1, 1863, Lincoln said that all slaves living in Confederate states were free. Soon after, Lincoln gave his famous speech, the Gettysburg Address. He honored those who had died during the Civil War.

- - - - - - - -

Una proclamación

El primero de enero de 1863, Lincoln declaró que los esclavos en los estados Confederados eran libres. Poco después, Lincoln pronunció su famoso discurso, llamado el Discurso de Gettysburg. En él, Lincoln honró a quienes habían muerto en la Guerra Civil.

17

Reelected

In 1864, Lincoln was elected president again. He saw this as a chance to free all slaves. Slavery was outlawed in 1865. Lincoln then met with Confederate leaders. He wanted them to end the war and rejoin the United States.

Reelección

En 1864, Lincoln fue reelegido presidente. Lincoln vio esto como una oportunidad para liberar a todos los esclavos. En 1865, se prohibió la esclavitud. Lincoln se reunió con los líderes de los estados Confederados. Lincoln quería acabar con la guerra y que los estados se unieran nuevamente a los Estados Unidos.

Lincoln's Death

John Wilkes Booth shot Lincoln on April 14, 1865. Lincoln died on April 15, 5 days after the war ended. Abraham Lincoln's leadership brought a country together. He helped end slavery. Lincoln's memory will always be honored.

- - - - - - - - - - -

La muerte de Lincoln

John Wilkes Booth le disparó a Lincoln el 14 de abril de 1865. Lincoln murió el 15 de abril, 5 días después del final de la guerra. El liderazgo de Lincoln unió al país y ayudó a acabar con la esclavitud. Lincoln siempre será recordado.

Timeline/Cronología

1809 — Abraham Lincoln is born./
Nace Abraham Lincoln.

1842 — Lincoln marries Mary Todd./
Lincoln se casa con Mary Todd.

1860 — Lincoln becomes president./
Lincoln es presidente.

1861 — The Civil War begins./
Comienza la Guerra Civil.

1864 — Lincoln is reelected./
Lincoln es reelegido como presidente.

1865 — The Civil War ends. Lincoln dies April 15./
Termina la Guerra Civil. Lincoln muere el 15
de abril.

Glossary/Glosario

civil war: a war between two groups within a country

elect: to choose for a position in a government

House of Representatives: one part of the US Congress. The Senate is the other part.

secede: to leave a country

slavery: the state of being "owned" by another person and forced to work without pay

---

Cámara de Representantes (la): rama del Congreso de EE.UU. La otra rama es el Senado.

elegir: ser seleccionado para una posición en el gobierno.

esclavitud (la): ser "propiedad" de otra persona y trabajar sin recibir pago.

Guerra Civil (la): una guerra entre dos grupos en el mismo país.

separarse: dejar de pertenecer a un país.

For More Information/Más información

Books/Libros

Krensky, Stephen. *The Emancipation Proclamation.* New York, NY: Marshall Cavendish Benchmark, 2012.

Rosenberg, Aaron. *The Civil War.* New York, NY: Scholastic, Inc., 2011.

Web Sites/Páginas en Internet

The Extraordinary Story of the Battle of Gettysburg

www.gettysburg.com/bog/bogstory/story1.htm

Find out more about the most famous battle of the Civil War.

National Geographic Kids: Abraham Lincoln

video.nationalgeographic.com/video/player/kids/history-kids/abraham-lincoln-kids.html

Watch a video and read about the life of Abraham Lincoln.

Publisher's note to educators and parents: Our editors have carefully reviewed these Web sites to ensure that they are suitable for students. Many Web sites change frequently, however, and we cannot guarantee that a site's future contents will continue to meet our high standards of quality and educational value. Be advised that students should be closely supervised whenever they access the Internet.

Nota de la editorial a los padres y educadores: Nuestros editores han revisado con cuidado las páginas en Internet para asegurarse de que son apropiadas para niños. Sin embargo, muchas páginas en Internet cambian con frecuencia, y no podemos garantizar que sus contenidos futuros sigan conservando nuestros estándares de calidad y de interés educativo. Tengan en cuenta que los niños deben ser supervisados atentamente siempre que accedan a Internet.

Index/Índice